# LIVING WELL
# BY DESIGN

# LIVING WELL BY DESIGN

## MELISSA PENFOLD

PRINCIPAL PHOTOGRAPHY
BY

ABBIE MELLE

VENDOME

NEW YORK · LONDON

# CONTENTS

# INTRODUCTION

DESIGN SHOULD MAKE PEOPLE HAPPY. WHATEVER TYPE OF SPACE you're decorating, there's nothing more uplifting than a home that engages the senses and reflects your personality. This book will help you make sense of what good design really means and master the basic decorating principles to create interiors that look and feel like home, speak to you, and boost your confidence and happiness. It will break down the fundamentals—sense of place, light and space, composition and balance, and pattern and texture—and, by opening the door to some of the world's most beautiful homes, it will demonstrate how to hit the mark every time you pull a room together. Finally, it will show you how to make elegance look effortless, with a focus on my country house, which is a constant reminder not to try too hard.

Great design creates great moods. People want their homes to look good, but the way it makes them feel is just as important. Everything that surrounds you affects you, so surround yourself only with things you love. Home is where the heart is, and a beautiful interior enhances well-being. Decorating is about self-expression and self-respect: your interior—and the way you layer furniture, objects, textiles, colours, and art—is unique to you.

To be beautiful, an interior doesn't need to be full of expensive furniture and art—quite the opposite. Ultimately, it is more important to find out what you like and what suits you. If you find a satisfying combination of space, light, colour, materials, and things, it will refresh your spirits and put a smile on your face.

Good taste doesn't cost anything extra; it's as easy and as affordable to get things right as it is to get them wrong. Remember, the more expensive a piece, the more useful and flexible it should be. Make every item work for its keep. There are certain things you shouldn't skimp on: big, comfy sofas; wicker chairs with large, plump cushions; stone or wood floors with a beautiful rug.

Our surroundings reflect what we think of ourselves, so surround yourself with the best you can afford. Even if you live in a shoebox, honour your presence in it. Make sure everything you put on show speaks to you and sends a positive message to others. "I care about myself; I have taste, and I'm not afraid to show it." Be proud of where you live.

Having written about the interior design industry for the past thirty years and worked for top brands and magazines all over the world, I understand the positive and negative effects an interior can have on your sense of well-being. When the magic ingredients are present, a thoughtfully designed interior can boost your mood and make you feel alive.

OPPOSITE: To add your personal stamp to your home, consider going to places that stock one-offs: high-end stores, auction houses, antiques shops, thrift stores, homeware boutiques, even hardware outlets. Perhaps you'll find a vintage commode with patina, antique chairs, a gilt mirror, an expressionist painting—things you've never seen anywhere else.

For most people, home is the heart of life and is defined by a variety of activities— cooking, eating, working, learning, exercising, washing, relaxing, entertaining, and sleeping. To live comfortably, everything must function properly in all these areas. Things that work well, look beautiful, evoke memories, and inject quality into everyday living have a profound effect on happiness: a beautiful table picked up in Provence, a contemporary, milky-toned Japanese ceramic bowl, an expressionist painting bought at a gallery in Los Angeles. Even white linen curtains filtering shafts of sunlight on windows overlooking a lush green landscape or perhaps out to sea will bring endless joy.

It's never about spending astronomical amounts of money to impress others and demonstrate how wealthy you are. Because in reality these places often don't function properly and are not very inspiring to spend time in. So many people overdo everything. It's about simplifying what you own.

You don't need to make a distinction between "good" and "everyday" things. Good glasses and plates should be used every day. Just because something was a wedding present or your grandmother owned it doesn't mean it must be good. A good piece is something that has great proportions, is well balanced, and is a joy to use. Look

*Everything that surrounds you affects you,*

*so surround yourself only with things you love.*

at everything you have without preconceptions and ask: What works best? What looks good? What do I like most? Expensive or not, these must be your everyday things.

Decorating is autobiography, and a home should always feel like a portrait of the person who lives there. Home is the ongoing story of a person and should be decorated with things that please the eye, soothe the senses, and move us in some way. It takes a lifetime of collecting to finish a room.

What stands out in today's interiors is freedom of expression, originality, rich eclecticism, and spirit—rooms filled with all kinds of pieces, whatever their provenance or value. Buy only what you love, and you'll be surprised how well everything works together over the years.

This book will help you learn to get things right the first time, have the confidence to make grand gestures, and get by with fewer but better things. Some of the strongest trends today are toward the decorative and the comfortable things that speak of intimacy, privacy, sensuality, and beauty.

Find things that make you happy, and you are more likely to enjoy your surroundings. Most important, they will allow you to live a more stress-free life, which is perhaps the greatest luxury in our increasingly chaotic times. A rule of thumb? Buy only things that you want around forever. But don't forget to throw a little curveball in from time to time.

OPPOSITE: Work with fabrics and textures to lighten the look of your home. Throw loose ecru cotton slipcovers over heavy chairs. Take up threadbare carpets and sand wood floors. Take down heavy curtains or blinds to let the light in. Arrange your flowers in the spot where they will be placed, so you can get the proportions just right. Look around your house for unused spaces and transform them into desirable— and functional—havens. In my house, I've added a window seat that hides storage underneath.

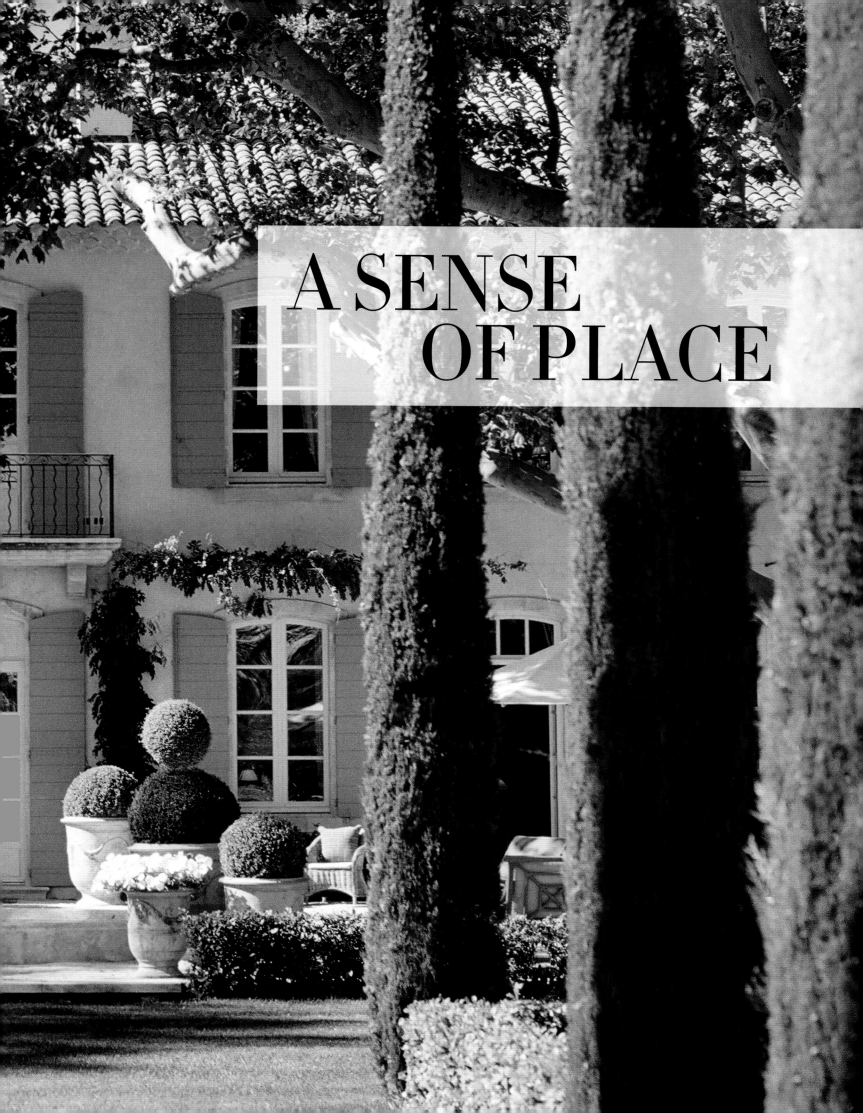

# A SENSE OF PLACE

A key aspect of creating a comfortable home involves discovering ways to amplify its sense of place. Following the latest fashions will not necessarily bring you happiness in your home, but embracing its setting certainly will.

You just need to open your eyes to the boundless possibilities of your house and its environment, and dedicate your energy to realizing its full potential. By linking your home to its setting, or by establishing a new narrative within the property's boundaries, you can create a place that feels special. It might sound like the sort of thing that only works if you live on a country estate or if your house looks like something out of *Architectural Digest*, but there are things that can be done wherever you live.

Suitability is everything. When designing your interior and exterior, your first thought should be: "Is this appropriate?" Play up the house's strengths. That might be its petite proportions, its light-filled, flowing spaces, or its sleek floor-to-ceiling door openings. Not to speak of the beautiful, borrowed views of hills or trees beyond. There can be no underestimating the importance of a home's relationship to its place, and its vistas are your greatest asset. The heady, full-on physical experience of a home is to be had only when you maximize its interaction with its setting.

When you are designing your house and garden, the aim is to create your own little world—a sanctuary—within your property's boundaries, a place that feels timeless and sits happily in its location, whether you live in an urban bedsit, a suburban flat, or a rural idyll. However small your home, don't underestimate its potential.

Open your windows. Nature is the original palliative. There's something about connecting with the natural world that makes the daily minutiae dissolve. Bring in more light, more air. We think the biggest bang for your buck is to open up a ceiling and extend door openings to outdoor spaces. It's not cheap, but it's life changing.

For others, it's simply a question of making use of what's already on their doorstep. Does your home sit beside water of some sort? A tranquil bay, a harbour, a lake, or a flash of river will create a focal point and distract the eye from other houses around you. A home that's intimately connected with its landscape will create a heart-stopping experience. There's no point living somewhere beautiful if you don't know how to make the most of it.

Keeping this sense of place in mind will imbue your home with a coherence that unites all the elements—decorating, landscaping, materials, and structure—so they work together as a whole, rather than leaping from genre to genre, or continent to continent.

Think about what you want. Or where you'd want to be. Do you sneer at minimalism and prefer a rustic farmhouse look? Are you partial to a curated, modern style or do you want to feel transported to an exotic clime? No matter what your preference, your first thought should be whether your concept is appropriate to the setting. Obsessively pruned parterre gardens and Louis XIV furniture look great at Versailles but wrong—even cheap—in and around a seventies' kit home. Who wants a Balinese cabana or a Tuscan villa on the twenty-third floor? If, for example, you yearn for a tropical garden, then espaliered fruit trees would look rather odd amid a mass of ferns and teak daybeds. The aim is for all elements to complement one another, from materials to colours, textures, and patterns, harmoniously. The idea is for home and garden to be united as one.

My house and garden look like they have been there forever. In fact, it has all been created in the past decade. I have kept things simple, using the same pale, muted palette and salvaged materials to layer the garden with references from the house and vice versa, all within a network of live climbing vines and towering verdant hedging bordering the property. Low box hedges are planted against the façade to anchor the house in the garden. You couldn't imagine any other house or garden in the space.

*Following the latest fashions will not necessarily bring you happiness in your home, but embracing its setting certainly will.*

For me, it's about screening out the world beyond, using vines, plants, fences, and trees to create an intimate space where there's no sense of the presence of neighbours. It's about building your garden around the architecture to make the house the heart of your property and using all the components in your garden to tell a cohesive story with no distracting flourishes.

In any interior, what is visible through the doors and windows is vital to expand the sense of space and blur the line between indoors and out. With the aid of natural light and vistas, you can make even a tiny place feel as big as the great outdoors. Houses where there always seems to be a fresh breeze will make you feel happy, confident, and as though you can endure almost anything. If you live in a city and crave a tranquil oasis to escape from your chaotic surroundings, consider adding a water feature—the ultimate garden luxury—such as a fountain or a reflecting pool to create a sense of serenity and mask the urban noise.

With our homes working harder than ever before, interiors will increasingly open to the outdoors to connect with nature. Forging a strong sense of place is fundamental to our happiness, health, and well-being. If we create more supportive havens for ourselves in which to live, we can weather the ups and downs of life. Your home has to be a refuge; as soon as you walk through the door, your spirits should lift. If it feels that way to you, everyone who lives there will be uplifted as well. That is the true purpose of home.

OPPOSITE: Your outdoor space should reflect your sense of style. If you want to be transported to the South of France when you step outside, aim for a gravel- or tile-paved patio, wooden garden furniture, and masses of terra-cotta pots. Many Provençal houses such as this one are blessed with old stone walls, which not only add warmth, incredible texture, and atmosphere but also provide a beautiful backdrop for the garden, with trees providing a canopy of shade for leisurely lunches.

RIGHT: Chateau St Victor La Coste in Provence is so organically integrated into the landscape that you can't imagine anything else in its place.

OVERLEAF: With its panoramic view of Sydney Harbour, the rooftop terrace of designer Lynda Kerry's former family home makes a perfect spot for drinks. Appointed with sofas by Eco Concepts and a coffee table by Robert Plumb, it echoes the design of the interior rooms in the choice of furniture, colour scheme, accessories, and even plantings.

OPPOSITE AND RIGHT: The table on the sun-soaked terrace at Australian designer Collette Dinnigan's Casa Olivetta in Puglia is shaded from the sun's harsh rays by a reed-covered pergola. Big or small, the most important design rules when you create a terrace are to pay attention to the scale of the available space and take advantage of existing features that can play the role of walls, floor, and ceiling.

OVERLEAF: To achieve a soft, romantic feeling around the swimming pool at Casa Olivetta, Dinnigan surrounded it with masses of flowering grasses.

RIGHT: No matter the size of your outdoor space, there are important lessons to be learned about garden design from landscape architect Dominique Lafourcade's garden at Le Mas des Poiriers in Avignon. A balance of texture, shape, and proportion is key. Evergreen trees and shrubs have year-round appeal and can create a sense of rhythm when planted in a series.

OVERLEAF: If you are fortunate enough to have a stunning view from your home, such as this vista from the remote Greek island of Symi, maximize it by creating an inviting patio, balcony, or terrace from which to enjoy it. This terrace was a ruin until architect Dimitris Zographos renovated it with mosaic paving based on ancient local techniques and built-in seating.

*In any interior, what is visible through*
*the doors and windows is vital to*
*expand the sense of space and blur*
*the line between indoors and out.*
*With the aid of natural light and vistas,*
*you can make even a tiny place*
*feel as big as the great outdoors.*

RIGHT: In this home with interior design by Victoria Hagan and landscape design by Joeb Moore & Partners, French doors and floor-to-ceiling windows bring the outdoors in, enhancing the décor and expanding the sense of space.

OVERLEAF LEFT: This house, designed by architecture firm McAlpine House, optimizes its connection to its urban location. Its windows look out on, and reflect, both the cityscape and the surrounding treetops. In lieu of a garden, planters filled with colourful flowers contribute a touch of natural beauty to the terrace.

OVERLEAF RIGHT: The sweeping mountain view through the double-height windows in the great room of a North Carolina home by architect James Carter enhances the elegantly cozy décor by interior designer Jane Hawkins Hoke.

PRECEDING PAGES: Every outdoor space and setting has its strengths, so make the most of yours. If you have a deck with an enviable sea view, such as this one on the Greek island of Serifos, arrange the seating so that it directs the eye to the vista.

RIGHT: At Wollumbi Estate, in the Southern Highlands of New South Wales, a gravel path punctuated by urns on plinths, lends a stately air to its garden.

OVERLEAF: The Boston ivy enveloping Wollumbi adds an extra layer of texture to the brick-clad residence. Houses wrapped in climbing vines always look "planted" in their setting.

# LIGHT AND SPACE

PRECEDING PAGES: In the
spacious kitchen of musician
John Mellencamp's retreat
on Daufuskie Island, South
Carolina, interior designer
Monique Gibson enlarged the
glass doors to flood the room
with natural light. The pale
palette and sparse furnishings
make the room look more
expansive. An Urban Electric
Co. lantern is suspended
above the kitchen table.

OPPOSITE: The windowpanes
in a pair of elegantly arched
doors handcrafted from
antique wood let the light into
the spacious entry of Sticks &
Stones, a house in Memphis,
Tennessee, by architect
Brad Norris and interior
designer Teresa Davis of Post
31 Interiors. A chandelier
by Currey & Company and
sconces by Visual Comfort
illuminate the hundred-year-old
ceiling beams and flooring
of the space, which doubles
as an entertaining area.

Our plugged-in culture has left us craving homes that welcome light and airiness—the sky, the sun, a breeze. We increasingly thirst for open windows, balconies, and terraces. Even a skylight offers a reprieve.

Light and space are intrinsically interwoven and connected. Yet each has its own impact, which can be maximized with the simplest of alterations to your surroundings. One of the easiest, but most dramatic, ways to upgrade an interior is to improve the quality of light. Flood a room with natural light and your spirits will soar straightaway.

The right light lifts the mood of a space, inspires productivity, and motivates us. We need space around us to appreciate the effects of light, and we need light to reveal space. Natural light, in particular, greatly affects the quality of any space. However small, a space that's suffused with natural light will feel amazingly calm and serene.

Sunlight helps almost any room look its best, but it's possible to have too much of a good thing. Direct natural light pouring through windows can be almost blinding and also fades artwork and textiles. Plus, if the windows look out on neighbouring apartments or homes, uncovered windows may make your space feel uncomfortably exposed. If that is the case, choose the window treatment—roller or roman shades, wooden venetian blinds, curtains, or shutters—that will work best with your architecture.

The aim of interior lighting is to mimic the patterns of daylight, which shifts as the sun moves across the sky over the course of the day and has a phenomenal impact on our circadian rhythms. Clever combinations of lighting, including ceiling lights, table and task lamps, and more decorative sconces, allow you to change the lighting for any given mood and time of day. Dimmable light switches in various parts of a room provide almost endless options for change. We also need darkness and coziness as well as bright light, so there should be areas of your house that are more snug and dimly lit.

Don't light up your house like a football stadium. Lighting is all about creating atmosphere. You want it to flatter you and your home, not show up every wrinkle and stain. Choose lights that make everyone look beautiful— seductive even. Soft light is magic. That's why so many marriage proposals are made during candlelight dinners. Layers of light are very important to create different focal points, so mix chandeliers, uprights, low pendants, and wall lights. Use spotlights to showcase great bookcases and art. Add table lamps for drama. Throw open the windows and doors, and roll up every blind to bring in natural light during the day. It will make everything just seem fresher. At night, do the opposite. Turn off overhead lights and create dimly lit pools of warm glow from lamps and candles.

Good lighting can make a difference in the appearance of the furniture, the walls, and the people in the room, so it's important to think about the quality and type of light. A poorly chosen fixture or a bulb that produces low-quality illumination can ruin even the most beautifully designed room. Powerful overhead lighting is the work of the devil, and unless you glue the dimmer switch to its lowest setting, the most well-designed interior will look like a shopping mall.

What attracts us to certain spaces and not to others has little to do with room size or sheer elbow room and more to do with proportions, balance, and character. The right quality of space puts us at ease. It's about the unity of space, the flow of each room into the other, the house as a harmonious whole. Openness and enclosure, togetherness and privacy—all are equally desirable and necessary.

---

*We need space around us to appreciate the effects of light, and we need light to reveal space.*

---

The quality of space plays a key role in our enjoyment of life, so it's important to make the most of the space you have. There are many well-designed small rooms that feel spacious yet intimate and efficient. Carve space out of every niche and optimize every alcove. Sliding doors save space, hide clutter, and give texture to a bland wall. Make every square metre work double time: a desk can be a wide ledge emerging from a bookcase or a section of kitchen island.

Variations in room scale are vital. Too many big, open-plan spaces can leave you at sea, whereas little rabbit warrens can be claustrophobic. But as anyone who has lived in a vast, open-plan home will tell you, we also need spaces that are small, secure, and private. Think of your rooms as a stage: there are areas that you want to accentuate and others that you want to fade away, depending on the time of day and your activities.

Most people do not in fact need more space; rather, they need fewer things, combined with a rethink of the space they have. The single best way to improve the look of a space is to take things out of it. If you don't use something, remove it from your life. That said, don't go minimal in a small space. A little room with nothing in it will always look like a little room with nothing in it, but clever decorating will result in a beautiful room with character.

Many homeowners desire an upgrade of some kind—additional rooms, an expanded kitchen, a massive rear extension—but the larger the house, the more likely that everyone will end up huddled together in one area, leaving the rest of the place empty. You don't need as much space as you might think to live well—just enough to accommodate the activities that make you happy. With a mix of lighting that sets the right atmosphere and spatial diversity, you'll be well on your way to creating rooms that are models of livable proportions, completely comfortable spaces to be in, live in, and socialize in.

OPPOSITE: In the dining area of actress Meg Ryan's former SoHo loft, designed by Monique Gibson, artist Dean Barger painted an elegant mural that enhances the room's dramatic mood. The dark walls are offset by the light pouring in through the window, reflected in the mirrored fireplace surround, and bouncing off the glossy table.

OVERLEAF LEFT: How can you make your home feel more light and airy? Start by opening your curtains or ditching them completely, as the owner of Wollumbi Estate did in this hallway between the master bedroom and bathroom.

OVERLEAF RIGHT: The master bathroom at Wollumbi is illuminated by a decorative chandelier that casts a subtle glow at night. It is positioned above an antique bathtub with brass fixtures.

*There are many well-designed small rooms that feel spacious yet intimate and efficient. Carve space out of every niche and optimize every alcove.*

RIGHT: Ideally, you should have more than one source of light in a room; think a layered mix of overhead, accent, and task lighting. In this kitchen designed by M. Elle Design, for example, there is a decorative pendant over an island, a floor lamp, and downlighting to gently wash walls and bounce light off the ceiling.

OVERLEAF LEFT: A wall of windows brings natural light into a room designed by Cathy Kincaid, increasing the sense of space and creating a visual connection between indoors and the garden.

OVERLEAF RIGHT: The wall of metal-framed windows and doors in this room designed by Rachel Halvorson not only makes the space brighter, lighter, and bigger but also lets the outside in, allowing the garden to have an aesthetic impact on the interior.

LEFT AND OPPOSITE: In this room at Wollumbi Estate, it's the subtle interplay between light and dark that creates visual appeal.

OVERLEAF AND PAGES 60-61: People often play it safe with scale and proportion in their homes, but if you're willing to take risks, push the envelope and go for larger windows and door openings, the results can be exciting. At Wollumbi, floor-to-ceiling windows on both sides of the main living room increase the sense of space and bring the outdoors in, creating a natural backdrop for the curated mix of eighteenth- and nineteenth-century French tables, commodes, mirrors, and statuary, as well as chandeliers and lamps handpicked in France.

TOP AND BOTTOM LEFT: Instead of hiding things away, the owner of Wollumbi fully embraced the concept of open shelving for pots, pans, and crockery in their kitchen.

OPPOSITE: One place where bright light is just as important as mood is the kitchen. In the French farmhouse–style kitchen at Wollumbi, the solid marble countertops are flooded with recessed lighting along ceiling beams and LED strips that run along the bottom of the upper cabinets—the easiest way to create evenly lit counters.

LEFT AND OPPOSITE: A large statement fixture such as the one over a dining table at Wollumbi serves as a focal point not only of the room but also of the view from adjoining rooms. As soon as night falls, lighting is the most decorative element. Avoid harsh lights and use dimmers or adjustable lamps whenever possible.

OVERLEAF: In the master bedroom at Wollumbi, the antique French furnishings—commodes, bedside tables, tapestry, and rug—are illuminated in the evening by antique lamps with bulbs that bathe the room in a golden glow. In the age of LEDs, not all light sources are equal. Some may appear more yellow than others. Some may maintain a constant colour as they are dimmed, whereas others will get warmer, like traditional incandescent bulbs. If one fixture casts a warm glow while another emits a cool, bluish-white light, the overall look will be unsettling. So don't skimp on your lamps, especially the bases. You'll have your lamps for life, so think of them as an investment. Just make sure to get the base-to-shade proportions right. Most people's shades are too small. If you're in doubt, go with the larger shade. Pick great bases in classic shapes crafted from stone, marble, ceramic, metal, or glass. Shades come in a range of materials, but card, linen, and silk are classic choices. The shapes of shades go through fashions, but a drum in the right proportions is timeless. Avoid gimmicks. The most classic colours are white, beige, chocolate, and black.

OPPOSITE AND ABOVE: With its dramatic vaulted ceiling, dormer windows, and quiet vibe away from the public rooms, the attic is well worth a makeover to provide more space, good views, and ample natural light. The owner of Wollumbi turned unused attic rooms, including this one, into inviting guest bedrooms.

OVERLEAF: In another guest bedroom at Wollumbi, a dormer window creates an ideal nook for a comfortable vintage leather armchair, and a four-poster metal bed from Restoration Hardware was fitted under the sloping ceiling, reminding us that just because a room is small, it doesn't mean the bed has to be.

OPPOSITE AND ABOVE: All that is needed to transform an awkward under-the-eaves space into a cozy reading or conversation spot is comfortable seating, a table, a mirror, and a lamp—wine racks are optional.

OVERLEAF: As the selection of antique French table and floor lamps in this attic apartment at Wollumbi illustrates, beautiful lamps impart elegance and gravitas to a space. An average-sized living room needs at least four, each casting a subtle pool of light. Many people try to get away with fewer lamps and higher wattage, but when it comes to wattage, less is more.

RIGHT: The kitchen of the attic apartment at Wollumbi is bathed in natural light during the day and illuminated by a chandelier at night. You might be surprised by what an elegant fixture can do to make a small room feel grand.

OVERLEAF: In designer John Derian's airy New York sitting room, a daybed and a pair of sofas by Derian for Cisco Brothers provide comfortable seating. Vintage Caucasian rugs cover the coffee table and slipper chair. Vintage textiles and Jeanette Farrier throws add warmth, comfort, and sensuality. A Peter Gee painting hangs to the right of the mirror.

LEFT: Layer the light. Don't expect a single ceiling fixture to create a welcoming environment. Designers typically install three types of lighting—ceiling fixtures, table lamps, and floor lamps—to highlight different parts of a room and offer pleasing ambient light that can be adjusted for different functions and times of day. In designer Suzanne Rheinstein's master bedroom, a floor lamp next to a tufted chair and a table lamp on a dresser next to the bed facilitate reading at night. Fabrics by Rose Tarlow and Claremont dress the custom iron bed frame. The bedding is by Julia B. Linens, and the Louis XVI-style settee and ottoman are upholstered in a Hazelton House print.

ABOVE: In this room designed by Atelier AM, positioning a table in a corner of two window walls, with a comfortable sectional sofa as seating, comes as close to dining alfresco as it gets without actual contact with the elements.

OPPOSITE: In a sunroom by Pursley Dixon Architecture, floor-to-ceiling windows bring natural light indoors, increasing the sense of space and creating a visual connection with the garden.

*Throw open the windows and doors, and roll up every blind to bring in natural light during the day. It will make everything just seem fresher.*

RIGHT: In the airy, open kitchen of designer Monique Gibson's historic Italianate townhouse in Manhattan's East Village, steel-framed windows and doors maximize light and space and blur the boundary between exterior and interior. An Axel Einar Hjorth chair is pulled up to a Pebble desk by Gal Gaon.

OVERLEAF LEFT: Steel-framed doors and windows expand the sense of space in a galley kitchen by designer Thomas Hamel. Pendant lights illuminate the room at night.

OVERLEAF RIGHT: Natural light brightens the kitchen of interior designer Bunny Williams's recently decorated two-bedroom apartment on an upper floor of a 1920s Gothic Revival building in New York. The cabinetry is painted a dark custom colour by Donald Kaufman Color, and the multicolour terrazzo floor by Durite has a fresh, modern look.

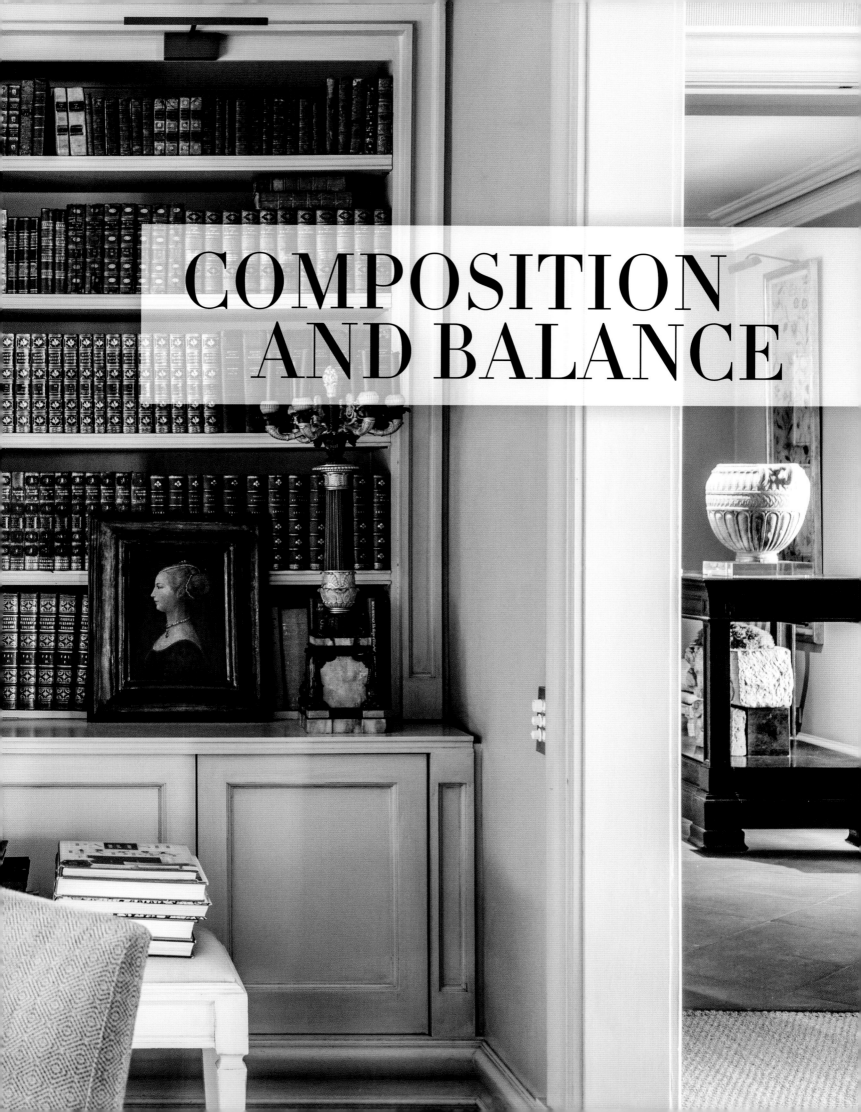

# COMPOSITION AND BALANCE

T he best interiors are a harmonious marriage between architecture and interior design, so before you start decorating, spend some time in your empty apartment or house. Get a feel for each room's proportions; register the quality and direction of light; and let the room's function dictate its design. Before you start furnishing the room, think about where each piece will go. Begin with the staples: sofas, chairs, dining table. Think of them as the equivalent of fashion's little black dress: the simpler and more classic they are, the more you can vary them with accessories. Buy the best you can afford. It's cheaper in the long run. The more beautifully made, understated, and timeless they are, the longer they will last and the more versatile they will be.

Give every room a focal point, something that creates visual interest or sparks conversation. When you arrange your layout, remember: even if you combine styles and periods with a wide variety of items, the curated look shouldn't lack focus. Accentuate an eye-catching element—it might be a fireplace, a rug, or a bold artwork. Rooms that are entirely colour coordinated feel unfocused; many paintings have a tiny dot of discordant colour somewhere to draw the eye, and so can your room.

As you determine your style, don't forget that the room is meant to be lived in. Let utility inform your decorating. When faced with an empty room, it can be daunting to make decisions about which furniture, objects, and colours to choose, but utility can be a great decorator. Think of how you use a room to help pull it together. After you've settled on the staples, consider baskets, bookshelves, drinks trays, and side tables. These elements lend a cozy, lived-in atmosphere to any space.

Make it a goal to find balance in scale and symmetry. Similar lines create design harmony, even if the pieces are of different styles and textures, or from different eras. Don't sacrifice organization for diversity. There's a fine line between layered/collected and busy/distracting. Good organization is invisible. Muddle stares you in the face. If everything has its proper place, it is more likely to be put away and found again in good condition.

Your individual style is characterized by a mix of things, and your choice of accessories like rugs, paintings, and objets d'art is a particularly telling way to express your personal aesthetic. They inject attitude and glamour, so don't skimp on them. Something French, something English, something Asian, even something kitschy often helps make a room distinctive. Remember, every single thing in a home has an energy level of its own, and everything must make a positive—and balanced—contribution to the whole.

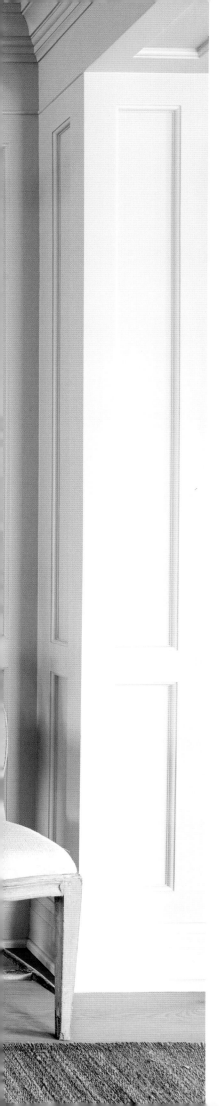

Create a variety of seating zones in a room to accommodate entertaining, reading, chatting, working, thinking, watching television. Don't use too many lone chairs in your living area—the room will seem unwelcoming and formal. Mix up different chair styles, along with ottomans. As Goldilocks found, dining chairs must not be too hard or too soft, and to be just right they must feel weighty—too light and no one trusts them. Nor should they be shiny or too futuristic.

Get rid of everything in your life that doesn't measure up, whether it's chipped cups or stained linens. Avoid matching sets of furniture, bath fittings, or bedroom suites; the most effective and affordable approach is to mix beautiful basics with one-offs. A sumptuous cushion elevates a plain sofa into the style stratosphere, a basic round metal table looks brilliant with an antique French chair. The most successful rooms defy categorization because they reflect their owner's individuality and life experiences.

Every room can benefit from accessories that have a history. The secret is to make sure your things are curated to maintain a sense of balance, unity, and structure; however eccentric each individual item, a well-arranged room will invariably be more than the sum

*Remember, every single thing in a home has an energy level of its own, and everything must make a positive— and balanced—contribution to the whole.*

of its parts. Even humble things like flowers and vegetables add balance to a room. Put parsley in a vase, grab a few pretty leaves from the garden. Foliage is the cheapest and chicest decorating accessory.

Throw a spanner into the works. The best rooms never take themselves too seriously, and the best houses never look spanking new, but comfortable, at ease, gently broken in. Learn to see the beauty in the everyday. Work on developing a good, strong eye. Don't get stuck in a time warp. The real test of a room's success is whether you spend time in it. If a room is gathering dust, change its function so you make use of it.

Show your individuality in your décor. To find the things that add your personal stamp, check out places that stock one-offs and collect things you've never seen anywhere else. In your hands, they tell the world, "I'm an individual. This is my taste."

ABOVE, OPPOSITE, AND OVERLEAF: Designer Thomas Hamel's former apartment in Sydney is an object lesson in achieving balance in colour, texture, and layout. The neutral-toned walls and furniture are contrasted by strong but not overpowering accent colours. The mix of materials and textures—linen, velvet, dark and wam-coloured wood—is also beautifully balanced. The floor plan is comfortably but not rigidly symmetrical.

LEFT: The size and placement of the furnishings and accessories in Hamel's former apartment complement, rather than compete with, one another. Find a piece you love, save up, take the plunge, and then build the whole room around it.

OVERLEAF: Your individual style is expressed in a multitude of fabrics, patterns, and accessories like rugs, paintings, objets d'art, and cushions, Keep in mind that it's all about balance, as the sitting room in designer Michael Love's longtime Sydney residence demonstrates.

OPPOSITE AND RIGHT: Strive for good lines, perfect proportions, and great finishes. Michael Love's Sydney sitting room is a reminder that successful room décor is all about achieving a pleasing composition of all the elements in it.

OVERLEAF: A beautiful glass screen in Michael Love's sitting room serves as a partition between the seating area and a study without blocking light.

OPPOSITE: When hanging art, composition, balance, and scale all come into play. The works should visually relate to the furnishings in the room, as well as to one another. Don't strand small works on a large expanse of wall; instead, group them together, as designer Vicente Wolf has done here.

RIGHT: Architect Joseph Dirand's understated Paris apartment is serenely composed. In the living/dining room, a work by Angel Alonso over the fireplace is teamed with a Le Courbusier cube, a sculpture by Nicolas Lefebvre, a light fixture and chair by Jean Prouvé, and a desk by Pierre Chareau.

OVERLEAF: Designer Axel Vervoordt opted for wide wood floorboards, a rustic plank ceiling, and warm wood cabinetry to transport the kitchen in director Ryan Murphy and photographer David Miller's Greenwich Village townhouse into the countryside.

LEFT: A sitting room designed by Tom Scheerer is an advanced lesson in how to get your furniture arrangement right. Give guests options to sit next to, opposite, or at right angles to each other, positioning a mix of sofas and chairs in a way that is pleasing both visually and psychologically. Don't place two sofas facing each other; it can be too confrontational. Create a natural path through the room at least one metre wide.

OVERLEAF: The wraparound seating and built-in bookshelves in the living room of the late travel writer Patrick Leigh Fermor and his wife Joan's famed villa in Kardamyli, Greece, look as fresh and inviting today as when the place was the venue for gatherings of royals and diplomats, writers and politicians. A good reminder to design wisely and well, to avoid making hasty or compromise decisions you'll later regret.

PAGES 114–15: The luxurious living room in designer Suzanne Rheinstein's Montecito home features a coffee table lacquered in Farrow & Ball's Mouse's Back in front of a custom sofa covered in a Victoria Hagan linen. The slipper chairs are upholstered in a Carolina Irving fabric and a Claremont fabric covers the eighteenth-century French chaise longue. The furniture arrangement—a mix of comfortable seating with good reading lights and handy tables to set drinks on—could serve as a blueprint, no matter where you live. Don't line up chairs against a wall as in a doctor's waiting room or all facing a big television. Remember, sofas never pull their full weight. A two-seater accommodates only one person comfortably; a three-seater, only two.

RIGHT: At John Mellencamp's South Carolina retreat, designed by Monique Gibson, wide steel-framed doors connect adjacent spaces to great theatrical effect. Gibson underscored the interconnection of the rooms by using the same materials and colours throughout: wood flooring, white walls, and industrial lighting.

OVERLEAF: A collection of glass vessels is beautifully displayed on the Mellencamp dining table. It's a reminder to never hide a beloved collection away but share it with the world. The enthusiasm you have for a collection is what keeps it alive. Group items together on a tabletop or shelf. Start with the biggest and best in the middle and work outward.

*As you determine your style, don't forget*
*that the room is meant to be lived in.*
*Let utility inform your decorating.*
*When faced with an empty room,*
*it can be daunting to make decisions*
*about which furniture, objects, and*
*colours to choose, but utility can be*
*a great decorator. Think of how you*
*use a room to help pull it together.*

RIGHT: To make this living room as relaxed—and functional—as possible, interior designer Carolyne Malone lined the walls with bookshelves and art, mixed up different styles of sofas, chairs, and tables, provided both overhead lighting and table lamps, and warmed it all up with pretty pillows and throws.

OVERLEAF: When director Ryan Murphy and photographer David Miller became the owners of the former chapel-like studio of Abstract Expressionist Hans Hofmann in Provincetown, they turned to interior designer David Cafiero to transform it into a guesthouse for entertaining and simultaneously protect Hofmann's legacy. Indeed, Hofmann's paint-splattered easel and stool grace a landing. Cafiero furnished the main room with an eighteenth-century chandelier, a pair of vintage Scandinavian wing chairs, a Scandinavian Deco sheepskin sofa, and a pair of leather armchairs by Le Corbusier and Pierre Jeanneret.

OPPOSITE: Interior designer Thomas Hamel knows that one of the first things people notice when they walk into a room is the window treatment. An expanse of gorgeous fabric in a pale tone makes a room seem larger and, when hung from ceiling to floor, even higher. Hamel often advises hanging curtains wider than the windows and being extravagant with the quantity of fabric (if you skimp on the amount, the result will always look, well, skimpy). Another Hamel tip is to go for muted background shades in carpets and walls and reserve stronger colours for chairs and accessories.

ABOVE: The kitchen in actress Meg Ryan's former SoHo loft, designed by Monique Gibson, has a classic, timeless look. It features symmetrical open shelving, industrial lights from a salvage shop in Maine, cabinets by Fine Woodwork, and a plank-top table by Get Back.

RIGHT: The Map Room in Martin Waller's Georgian country home in West Sussex, England, is wrapped in an atmospheric, sepia-toned wallpaper made from an ancient Chinese map. Chinese artifacts share the space with leather and wicker furniture, paintings resting on the floor, and a big rhino on the coffee table produced by Liberty in the 1960s. Everything looks a little battered and well used, full of patina and steeped in history.

OVERLEAF: As Martin Waller's house illustrates, every room can benefit from incorporating objects that have personal meaning into the décor. The trick is to curate and display your collection so that it has the balance, unity, and structure of a mini installation. Waller transformed the entrance hall into a cozy sitting area by filling the shelves with a collection of antique French ceramic vessels and the rest of the room with assorted urns, animal figures, and even a buffalo skull, all in a palette of chalky whites and creams.

# PATTERN AND TEXTURE

PRECEDING PAGES: Master the mix. In the upstairs study of designer Michael Love's Sydney home, a rich French antique tapestry elevates a linen sofa into the style stratosphere, a plain card lampshade looks brilliant beside a mounted fossilized artifact. The most successful rooms defy categorization because they reflect their owner's individuality and life experiences.

OPPOSITE: A beautiful bedroom is one of life's greatest pleasures. In the master bedroom of fashion designer Tory Burch's Southampton home, the George III–style four-poster bed is dressed in crisp white D. Porthault linens. The headboard and a great chair are upholstered in a classic Colefax and Fowler chintz, the colours of which are echoed in the framed botanical prints by Renzo Mongiardino. A Manufacture Cogolin hand-woven rug on the geometrically patterned floor adds texture.

Texture and pattern make interiors warm, welcoming, and comforting. Rooms with all matching curtains, cushions, and carpets, however upmarket, lack character. But a mix of textures, patterns, finishes, and colours infuses interiors with richness and depth.

Get the broad strokes right first. A rule of thumb is to pick a palette and work within it, using different textures and patterns in the same colour family. The pleasing combination of chalky, matte paintwork, nubbly linen and canvas, robust wooden floorboards, and woolen throws will be tonally similar but authentic and natural.

If you want your space to feel more luxurious, think of layering it with curtains, throws, rugs, and cushions that can soften hard architecture lines. Each of these layers and textures absorbs sound, makes a room feel rich, and promotes comfort.

Stick to muted or neutral background colours for floors and walls, then introduce favorite accessories in a variety of textures and patterns for dramatic contrast. Rattan trays, ceramic plates, books, tribal artifacts, Regency decanters, straw hats, or copper moulds are personal touches that add character and visual interest to a room. If you've got a huge collection, don't hide it away like a secret vice; share it with the world! Display the items in big, bold groups; don't dissipate their effect by scattering them around. Hang them on a wall, line them along shelves, assemble them on a tabletop. Aesthetically grouped, your collection will give your house soul—and lots of texture.

Textural quality contributes greatly to the pleasure we get from everyday activities: smooth glassware that feels good in the hand and on the lip, quality dinner plates that are a joy to eat from, cutlery that is satisfying to hold, polished floorboards that feel soothing underfoot. Steer clear of anything that isn't pleasing to the touch: fabrics, rugs, glasses, towels all have to pass the rub test. Pick things up and check the weight and the way they feel.

Decorating is like dressing: you can carry anything off if you have confidence. If you love the pattern or texture of a particular fabric, don't just use it on a cushion; cover a whole wall or sofa with it. If you're not sure of a texture or pattern, bone up on fabrics, finishes, materials, and colours. Learn to trust your eye, not the brand or price tag. Once you've made the big choices, the rest depends on how you put it together.

Pair the unexpected. Mix up your genres. Contrast textures: put cotton with silk, linen with velvet, and canvas with cashmere. Opposites attract; when paired, they reinvent themselves. Mix incongruous elements: upholster a French nineteenth-century painted-wood chair in an unpretentious gingham or team a white laminate table on a pedestal base with a

couple of antique Irish library chairs. On your travels, hit the stately homes; they're object lessons in how to pull different patterns and textures together into a harmonious whole.

Unity in colour is important when using different textures. Go for harmony and let each room in your home complement the others. Carry harmony throughout your home to create flow. Your interior will look disjointed if the textures, patterns, and styles change abruptly from one room to the next.

Keep it real. Choose natural fabrics over synthetics, authentic old furniture over reproductions, a cane laundry basket over a plastic one. Humble materials like hemp, rattan, cane, and jute can have a huge impact to a space without feeling trendy or overdone. They can also be paired with more luxurious pieces for a high-end look. Not everyone can inherit or afford antiques, but cheap reproductions look second-rate even to the untrained eye. A battered and weathered piece with a history has style simply because it's real. But then so does an object that is unapologetically modern: it will always speak authentically of the age in which it was made.

*Decorating is like dressing: you can carry anything off if you have confidence. If you love the pattern or texture of a particular fabric, don't just use it on a cushion; cover a whole wall or sofa with it.*

Texture can soften or sharpen a room. You only have to think about the difference between matte, satin, and gloss paint finishes. Paint is the most common and least expensive way to finish walls, but there are a number of alternatives that can add desirable textures. Specialty matte plasters with integral colours can give walls an earthy, rough appearance and a stone-like feel that is very calming. Though busily patterned wallpaper may not be ideal, grasscloth adds a natural touch to rooms and comes in many colours.

Be realistic about the way you live; there's no point making everyone's life miserable by choosing cream silk in a house full of children and dogs. If you're on a budget, use special fabrics for small pieces that make a big impact (stools, a great chair, cushions, headboards) and less expensive fabrics for curtains and sofas. But always use the best quality fabrics you can afford—it's money well spent.

The floor is one of the most expansive—and expensive—surfaces in a home and should be your first consideration when deciding on texture and pattern. Remember, flooring outlives paintwork, so it's best to stick to a natural surface that will work with successive colour schemes.

Pattern and texture dress our rooms, bringing beauty and comfort to our lives. Light or heavy, the textures and patterns you choose should always have some kind of affinity with one another to give a room a cocooning quality. Use the best you can afford—it will serve you well.

OPPOSITE: Don't be afraid to go bold. The striking black-and-white-striped walls and ceiling of this California loggia designed by Mark Rios has great impact. Strategic use of the same pattern for the curtains, bolsters, and sun chair, contrasted by the bright green fabric on the sofa and chairs, adds to the drama.

ABOVE: In this restoration of an early eighteenth-century farmhouse in Connecticut, the Eilish van Breems design team preserved the natural materials of the period: rough-hewn ceiling beams, plastered walls, and lime-washed wide plank floors. The room is furnished with some of the firm's finest antique Scandinavian pieces.

OPPOSITE: Designer Thomas Hamel prefers to use texture to build a room's character, reserving pattern for smaller accessories, which are potent but portable. In this room, the textured materials include linen, wood, crystal, gilt, silk, glass, silver, sisal, and matte paint, all of which feel good to the touch and won't date.

OVERLEAF: Australian designer Collette Dinnigan went easy on pattern in the living area of Casa Olivetta, her Puglia retreat, limiting it to the blue-and-white ticking covering the sofa cushions.

*Get the broad strokes right first.*
*A rule of thumb is to pick a*
*palette and work within it,*
*using different textures and*
*patterns in the same colour family.*

**PRECEDING PAGES:** In the entry hall at Wollumbi Estate, texture reigns: stone flooring, metal table and balustrade, vintage stick chair and pitchfork, and chopped firewood stored in floor-to-ceiling shelves bookending an antique French stone fireplace.

**RIGHT:** For his renovation of the kitchen in the mid-nineteenth-century Captain Osborne Edwards House in Sag Harbor, designer Steven Gambrel paired marble countertops and cool blue-grey walls with warm wood floors and cabinetry. The effect is both soothing and inviting.

**OVERLEAF LEFT:** In a decorative tour de force, designer John Derian arrayed his extensive collection of eighteenth-, nineteenth-, and twentieth-century dishware (including some of his own design) on open shelves in his New York kitchen.

**OVERLEAF RIGHT:** In his rustic retreat in the French countryiside, antiques dealer Robert Montagut layered pattern on texture, matching the crumbling walls' intensity with an antique tapestry and wooden overdoor. Mix incongruous elements. Throw in something unexpected. Recognize the beauty in the patina of time.

OPPOSITE AND ABOVE: Patterns and textures abound in designer Lynda Kerry's master bedroom. Vintage rattan and leather luggage top an old chinoiserie cabinet; batik textiles team with a bamboo chair; animal-print pillows decorate a tufted-leather bench; an oriental rug is layered over seagrass carpeting; and brown grasscloth walls above white paneled wainscoting tie the diverse elements into a harmonious whole.

OVERLEAF LEFT AND RIGHT: Designer Michael Love's study offers a great lesson in colour coordination. Every object in a room adds its colour "note." Decide on an accent colour and echo it in flashes: a chair, a vase, a cushion. Keep other colours to a minimum, so that your accent colour strikes its distinctive note.

PAGES 150–51: For a guest bedroom, Lynda Kerry chose a patterned Quadrille wallpaper as a starting point and decorated the room around it, keeping to the same colour family in different textures.

PRECEDING PAGES, OPPOSITE, AND ABOVE: African, Chinese, Indian, and Thai art, textiles, and furniture mix in the open-plan living/dining room of designer Lynda Kerry's former Sydney home. Wood melds with leather, lacquer, stone, antiqued mirror, rattan, sisal, ikat, cotton, porcelain, bone inlay, and greenery. The reason these disparate styles, patterns, and textures work together so seamlessly is a strict colour scheme of white, brown, and black, with blue as the primary accent colour.

PRECEDING PAGES: Robust textures and patterns have personal meaning for designer Lynda Kerry and her husband, Mark Kerry, a former Olympic swimmer, whose former house was a modern concrete box. She believes that a home should tell your story, reflecting the places you've travelled and the things you love. The casual sitting room is decorated with textiles and furnishings of different styles: African tribal cushions, Chinese ceramic table lamps, Indian metal lanterns, Indonesian wicker seating, American bamboo side tables, and an assortment of collectibles and mementos, as well as a portrait of her polo-loving husband.

OPPOSITE AND ABOVE: In this airy, light-filled entrance hall designed by Thomas Hamel, a bold, classic black-and-white chequerboard-patterned marble floor grounds the Asian-inflected décor.

*Unity in colour is important when using different textures. Go for harmony and let each room in your home complement the others. Carry harmony throughout your home to create flow.*

LEFT: In the dining room of a New York apartment designed by Tom Scheerer with the architect Gil P. Schafer, the boldly patterned rug by Allegra Hicks and the black walls combine to create a dramatic ambience, illuminated by a pair of Isabelle Sicart ceramic uplights atop custom columns. The colours of the rug are picked up in the Regency chair cushions, custom embroidered by Penn & Fletcher.

ABOVE AND OPPOSITE: Discover the magic of hanging art the right way. In the master bedroom of designer Michael Love's Sydney residence, he has grouped a collection of architectural drawings on the dark walls, which make the works pop and pull out their inky shades. Photos in gleaming frames are amassed on a bedside table, giving the room added soul.

OVERLEAF: A guest bedroom in designer Collette Dinnigan's Casa Olivetta in Puglia illustrates how the use of a single colour can serve as a unifying factor and create a cohesive look.

*Pattern and texture dress our rooms,*

*bringing beauty and comfort to our lives.*

*Light or heavy, the textures and patterns*

*you choose should always have*

*some kind of affinity with one another*

*to give a room a cocooning quality.*

RIGHT: The rules for devising a colour scheme are simple. First establish your base, or main background, colour for the room, as in this kitchen designed by Steven Gambrel. Then choose a second, related colour, and finally an accent colour to add drama in small touches. As a rule, use the strongest colour in the smallest amount. Matte trims are more desirable than gloss, which tends to show dust and chips readily; satin enamel is best.

PRECEDING PAGES LEFT: The textures in John Derian's kitchen are as charming and eclectic as his signature decoupaged tableware. Pendants by Robert Ogden hang over the island, and a nineteenth-century diorama is mounted above an antique sink.

PRECEDING PAGES RIGHT: Everything in the kitchen at Casa Olivetta, designer Collette Dinnigan's vacation house in Puglia, is pleasingly tactile, from the the ancient stone ceiling and stone floor to the tile backsplash, sturdy wooden island, and her collection of Italian hand-painted ceramic tableware.

RIGHT: The renovated galley kitchen in a classic New York prewar apartment could not be widened, but it was given a modern facelift by designer Elizabeth Bauer Watt and architect Sam Mitchell. They installed sleek, black-lacquered cabinetry, marble and chrome finishes, and a floor custom painted in a chequerboard pattern by JJ Snyder Studio.

OPPOSITE: In the breakfast room of a New York apartment designed by Tom Scheerer, the walls, papered in 1890s botanical prints by João Barbosa Rodrigues, set both the cheerful mood and the colour scheme.

ABOVE: In the nearby kitchen, Scheerer covered the walls in subway tile crowned by a floral wallpaper frieze. All of the cabinetry is custom. The billiard-style pendant over the island is from Ann-Morris, the flooring is by APC Cork, and the walls are decorated with decoupaged trays by John Derian.

OVERLEAF: For a sitting room at Woody House in East Hampton, architect and interior designer Peter Marino designed custom textiles, reworked Indian cotton prints into slipcovers, and dressed Austrian-style horn chairs in a paisley chintz, mixing big and small patterns, designed the painted "rug," and teamed stripes with trellis motifs, old with new, smooth with rough.

OPPOSITE: In colour and finishes, Steven Gambrel pulled out all the stops for a knockout kitchen in Greenwich Village. The bespoke elements include a mosaic-tiled vaulted ceiling, marble backsplash and countertops, Art Deco pendants, grey-lacquered cabinets, an aubergine La Cornue range, and brass, bronze, and chrome accents.

ABOVE: When asked to renovate a 1929 Dallas estate, architect Peter Marino reworked the interior completely, but it's impossible to tell the old from the new because he used only materials that had been used in the house originally, such as the limestone for the walls of this entrance. The console, however, was designed by his firm.

# FROM A HOUSE TO A HOME

Ten years ago, while driving in the Australian countryside, my husband and I chanced upon this house on an autumn afternoon. We weren't really looking for a country place but didn't hesitate for a moment. Like most things, as soon as we set eyes on it, we knew. A few weeks later, we owned it. It was as though the house found us.

The house is located in a small, picturesque village about 140 kilometres from Sydney, in Australia's Southern Highlands. We bought it as the ultimate country escape from our busy city lives, set amid fruit trees, hedges, and lawns that give onto endless horizons.

The district is reassuringly familiar; it's where my family has holidayed for generations, owned rural properties, and attended boarding schools. We lived in Sydney, but my mother and father had a 500-acre property in the area that I loathed visiting—I wanted to stay in the city. It's also where my husband and I met at a country wedding. Now, green space has become far more appealing.

The house, barn, and stables were built by skilled local hands about a decade ago, using old architectural pieces salvaged from around the world. The main house feels old because it has serious quantities of reclaimed French oak parquetry flooring, soaring salvaged windows and stone fireplaces, plus old timber doors. All have a history and patina that is great to look at and live with. I didn't spend a fortune decorating the place. I did what I always do and went with the house instead of changing it. A lot of things, including the paint colours, wallpaper, and curtains, I wouldn't have chosen, but I'm a great believer in using what you've got.

I build rooms around collections, not fabric swatches. If you buy things you love and throw them together well, a room will work. Then I dusted off the cheque book and went shopping for a couple of key pieces.

I opted for timeless staples that can be mixed and matched. A couple of pretty chairs and tables, a good mirror, elegant new table lamps, and an antique tapestry. They are all high-quality, fad-free classics that we can take through life and will last the distance. I am a big believer that glamorous accessories can give a fresh look and will cost a lot less than a complete overhaul.

Next, I had new slipcovers whipped up in plain, tough, off-white canvas to lighten up old sofas, armchairs, and cushions. It was like putting them in summer frocks. They dramatically altered the rooms, bringing harmony to discordant pieces of furniture and

making everything relaxed and elegant—all at a fraction of the cost of reupholstering them. Plus, we can pop the slipcovers in the washing machine. Other key pieces are an ottoman covered in a Fortuny damask and antiques bought with some of my first pay cheques: a nineteenth-century French mirror, an Irish Gainsborough reading chair, a Georgian Pembroke table. I had built up a good collection as a young married woman, so I had staples that I could move from house to house. Accessories range from more traditional paintings to African shields on the mantelpiece to foliage and vegetables.

I brought a touch of glam to bedrooms and bathrooms with big, new, fluffy white cotton towels and crisp hotel sheets throughout. I dug out old wicker baskets and vases to display fruit and leaves.

When it comes to easy living, I focus on simple pleasures that bring joy to daily life. At the beginning of each week, I grab big bunches of pretty leaves from the garden, sticking to one or two types like magnolia, laurel, or bay for maximum impact. I put inexpensive bunches of kale in jugs, frilly lettuces in teapots, onions in bowls, cauliflower in urns. I love the beauty of nature in all its forms. Florist arrangements might be great, but I prefer mine to be spontaneous, natural, and authentic. I've usually got no time to arrange,

*This house is about celebrating the art of living and knowing that the chicest thing of all is to be true to yourself. The rooms are elegant, warm, and welcoming but also humble.*

so I go for quantity: thirty apples or potatoes in a basket packs ten times the punch. I fill trays with big, knobby lemons with their leaves attached from a tree in the garden. Nothing could be simpler.

Life in this house is uncomplicated and undemanding—the vibe most people seek from a holiday. We enjoy beautiful surroundings, simple pleasures, and good food. Fresh coffee, bowls of fruit, loaves of bread, a glass of wine, slabs of cheese. The interior feels like a still-life painting; all the elements are in harmony.

This house is about celebrating the art of living and knowing that the chicest thing of all is to be true to yourself. The rooms are elegant, warm, and welcoming but also humble. I prefer rooms that are relaxed to the point of almost being "un-decorated."

One of the greatest compliments I can get is when visitors throw off their jackets and feel as relaxed in our surroundings as my family and I do. It isn't completely accidental: the pleasure derives from the combination of comfort, simplicity, and practicality. It's something anyone can achieve.

How and where we live is fundamental to our well-being. The house is proof that you can really get a new look for a whole lot less money than you think. Great decorating is not about spending a fortune. It's about knowing where to scrimp and where to spend, getting the mix right, and understanding that style should never hijack comfort.

OPPOSITE: Moving a table around the garden expands the areas for pleasant alfresco meals.

Books are central to all my houses, the ultimate finishing touches. I use them like works of art, stacked up high on tables, and change them regularly. They are decorative, interesting, and great company.

My homes are always a mix of things from all times and places, from grand to simple. I choose natural fabrics over synthetics, authentic furniture over reproductions, something battered and weathered with a history that has style simply because it is real. And I buy only pieces that are well made, do their job properly, look great, and bring pleasure to everyday living. The more understated the piece (and room), the longer it will last.

In line with my mantra, "Keep it simple," I went for beiges, butterscotches, khakis, soft greens, and blues sharpened with black—a foolproof palette—and then I layered in my beloved collections. There are a lot of wicker trays, potted cyclamen, glass hurricane lamps, and cabbage-ware plates—all classic pieces to cherish forever. For me the recipe for a beautiful country home is straightforward; the ingredients include a

*The main house feels old because it has serious quantities of reclaimed French oak parquetry flooring, soaring salvaged windows and stone fireplaces, plus old timber doors.*

lot of mirrors, a few really good pieces of furniture, whopping beds with crisp white linens, and generous bunches of foliage to lend a feeling of country splendour. It's very simple, but it works.

The most important thing is that the house is very easy to live in. In addition to being warm and textural, it works. The joys are many: spending time in a bathroom with radiant heating underfoot, for example, or cooking with a decent oven. Luxuriating in the gentle warmth of flat-panel radiators. Reading on a really comfortable sofa next to a crackling fire. Enjoying little details such as a walk-in pantry, self-closing drawers that shut silently, and solid door hardware that feels good in the hand. Objects that get used daily need to be not only good-looking but durable and serve the purpose that you bought them for. And you should never skimp on the things you use every day.

The house and barn are covered seasonally in clematis, roses, wisteria, and Boston ivy. The terrace that opens off the living room faces a wall covered in lattice-patterned star jasmine. We eat out there eight months of the year. It's so peaceful.

It is first and foremost a family home, but it is also where I work, so it's a centre of creative energy. It's where we entertain, too; the house loves a party and loves people. In the beginning, it was very much a weekender, but now it's become our full-time home. And it's the happiest house. It's just easy to live well here, and at the end of the day, living well is what it's all about.

OPPOSITE: Don't put things in glass boxes—you're a homemaker, not a curator. Turn your collections into décor. In the foyer, coral, pencils in pots, small antique boxes, and Colefax and Fowler lacquered dishes are grouped on an antique French tabletop, starting with the biggest and best in the middle. Rubber boots are piled in a vintage basket.

OPPOSITE: The entry sets the stage and vocabulary for the whole residence. A round black neoclassical 1920s table surrounded by wicker armchairs is usually topped with a basket filled with bunches of garden leaves. Foilage is one of the quickest ways to soften architecture, add a focal point, and make a space look lived in.

RIGHT: A black chinoiserie cabinet beautifully resonates with the table in the entry. A canvas slipcover freshens up an antique French stool, and a geometrically patterned Dash & Albert jute rug anchors the room.

OVERLEAF: Salvaged French oak parquetry flooring underpins everything in the main living area. Flooring has the biggest impact on any room's aesthetics, practicality, and budget. You can sit on a box on a beautiful floor and be happy, but nothing will ever improve a cheap floor. The space features a mix of sofas and chairs that are good both visually and psychologically, with plenty of upright and sprawling options to suit all inhabitants and guests.

PAGE 190: In rooms that don't need privacy, dispense with curtains. Having bare windows is a great way to make a room feel airy. We all need as much sunlight as possible. No window treatments are better than bad window treatments.

PAGE 191: How you organize your books says a lot. Collections of hardcover volumes stacked on a coffee table not only look great but also are easily accessible.

**OPPOSITE AND RIGHT:** Once you've got your interior structure (walls and floors) right, layer your interiors with staples and accessories. About 70 percent of a room should consist of classic staple pieces—tables, sofas, chairs, commodes, bookcases, mirrors—that don't date. The other 30 per cent can be favorite accessories (think "home jewellery"). Choose the best you can afford. Quality pays long-term dividends and will provide a lifetime of enjoyment.

**OVERLEAF LEFT AND RIGHT:** Play with your furniture arrangement. A big mistake people make is leaving the layout of a room the same as it was when they first moved in. Everyone who thinks there's only one right furniture arrangement is wrong. By moving a bookcase, a commode, or a pretty chair, you might experience the room in a totally different way, as I did when I took a chair out of the bedroom and placed it beside a red secretaire near the fireplace (right).

PRECEDING PAGES: The bedroom sets your mood at the start and end of every day, so turn it into a haven. We like ours to be soft and beautiful; it's our most powerful ally in pursuit of well-being. When it comes to the bed, position it with care, giving it pride of place in the room, most likely with the headboard positioned against one wall and paths for walking on both sides. Get the height right. Beds that are less than 60 centimetres off the ground make a room look like student digs. Move up in the world—as high as 76 centimetres off the ground—and you'll elevate the entire room. The aim is to have it facing something appealing, which could be as simple as a painting on the wall or, if the architecture allows, a window. Items we love are displayed to meet the needs of the soul. A freshly dressed bed is one of the finer things in life, and yet many stumble here. For harmony, work with your overall colour scheme. The colours do not have to be identical to those in the rest of the room, but they do need to be similar in tone. For the bedding, we prefer four standard-size pillows stacked with a pair of European pillows, a down duvet, and a coverlet or quilt folded at the foot of the bed. You want to create a place for slumber that looks beautiful, yet also cultivates a state of serenity.

OPPOSITE AND RIGHT: Your enthusiasm for everything from vintage copper cookware to cabbage-ware plates and cake stands is what keeps a collection alive, so don't hide objects away in a cupboard. Group items together in one place. Remember, if it's worth collecting, it's worth displaying well. The more individual your tastes, the more interesting your collection will be. It's also a really good way of decorating: a kitchen island covered with copper pots, a countertop filled with pretty bowls, walls covered with traditional French art. Love your collection for itself, not its dollar value.

PRECEDING PAGES: Whenever possible, open the doors and let the daylight in to blur the boundary between indoor and outdoor spaces. Fill the receptacles you have—vintage baskets, crockery, decanters, and even ice buckets—with seasonal flowers, greenery, and fruit to decorate tables. Interiors are as much about "feel" as "looks." Turn your collections of china or glassware into décor. Raid your cupboards and layer your table with lovely plates, vases, stands, and trays. The effect will be so entrancing that guests won't want to leave.

OPPOSITE: Boston Ivy covers the entire south façade of the house for much of the year, adding to the greenery in the garden and making it look like our relatively new house goes way back. We try to liven up the outdoors (and entertaining) by rethinking our use of the space we have; we have even set up a table in the driveway.

RIGHT AND OVERLEAF: When the clematis is in bloom, we utilize the barn as a backdrop for a table setting at dusk. Upgrades to one's home and garden tend to involve expansions of some sort: additional rooms, a bigger garden. We do not in fact need more space, just a rethink of the space we have and how to use it in new ways.

*For my lovely children, Isabella and Hugo*

# ACKNOWLEDGMENTS

A few individuals played a major role in making this book happen. My thanks go first to publisher Mark Magowan, who urged me into the project with an unexpected email back in July 2019, saying he had discovered me on Instagram, greatly admired my work, and would like nothing more than to find a way for me to write for Vendome. Throughout, Mark has been hugely generous with his advice, support, and guidance, and many of his suggestions elevate the book. Jackie Decter, my editor at Vendome, is a marvel, shepherding the book at every stage, turning text into treasure, spotting what's missing, and becoming a New York friend. They knew the book better than I did, and the work became an enjoyable collaboration. I have also been greatly supported by my clever daughter, Isabella, a shining light in my life, who rallied around to help with the book from beginning to finish, providing a sharp, critical eye, as only family can do. There really aren't enough words to thank her.

Thank you, Susi Oberhelman, for the book's exceptional design because, let's face it, looks matter. Photo research was easy thanks to Karen Howes's tireless sourcing efforts. Thanks to the gorgeous Lisa Fine, who provided the beautiful fabric for the cover. Her textiles make everything look good. And of course, a big thank you to delightful photographer Abbie Melle; I simply love working with you.

I'd like to thank every single house owner, architect, and designer whose homes are featured in the book, particularly Michael Love, Thomas Hamel, Collette Dinnigan, and the owner of Wollumbi Estate, who are friends and know I have no shame asking for help.

Mostly I want to thank my family, who played a big role in developing my early interest in design. My parents had a number of houses in Australia, and my mother had incredible taste. I grew up in a house decorated by the influential decorator Marion Hall Best, renowned for her bold colour, lustrous surfaces, and va-va-voom rooms, and both of my grandmothers had fabulous houses. My mother's mother had an extraordinary harbourside residence with a ballroom and one of the country's first residential lifts. The house won design awards and was on the cover of the top magazine of the day. Both my mom and her mother were extravagant women—I think I've had a reaction against them with my cheap "salad décor." They often took me antiquing and to the leading department stores at the time, giving me incredible exposure to art, antiques, and design.

My thanks as well to my first husband's family, the Walker-Smiths, who had a truly beautiful home, decorated by another famous Australian interior decorator, Merle du Boulay, who also designed my paternal grandparents' house. Du Boulay was renowned for sherry-coloured backdrops, which she mixed with accents of pink and lime. Most of the furniture in these houses was painted a matte beige. The décor really resonated with me, filling me with calm.

The lesson I learned from my family was to be proud of where you live. You must keep your standards up. Most people know how to live, but not how to live well. They might have the money, but they don't have the know-how. They know how to spend, but not how to shop. They know how to furnish a room, but not how to decorate. There is a world of difference between the two—and the difference is style. For this lesson, I am forever grateful. It's such a great way to live.

MELISSA PENFOLD

# PHOTO CREDITS

All photographs by Abbie Melle, with the exception of the following:

François Dischinger/Trunk Archive: 2–3 | Julia Klimi: 6–7, 32–33, 38–39, 112–13 | Oliver Fly: 16–17, 30–31 | David Tsay/OTTO: 19 | Monica Spezia/Living Inside: 20 | www.chateau-st-victor-la-coste.com: 22–23 | Paul Raeside/OTTO: 26, 27, 28–29, 138–39, 164–65, 169 | David Sundberg/Esto: 34–35 | Werner Straube: 36 | Annie Schlechter/Interior Archive: 37, 83, 120–21 | William Abranowicz/Art + Commerce: 44–45, 48, 84–85, 118–19, 125 | Emily Minton Redfield: 47 | Shade Degges: 52–53 | Tria Giovan: 54 | Paige Rumore Messina: 55 | Stephen Kent Johnson/OTTO: 78–79, 108–9, 122–23, 144, 168 | Laura Resen: 80–81, 114–15 | François Halard/Trunk Archive: 82 | Nick Watts: 86 | Reid Rolls: 87 | Richard Powers: 92–93 | Anson Smart: 94, 95, 96–97, 124, 137 | Matt Lowden: 98–99 | Fritz von der Schulenburg/Interior Archive: 106 | Adrien Dirand: 107 | Francesco Lagnese/OTTO: 110–11, 160–61, 170–71, 172, 173, 174–75 | Edward Addeo: 116–17 | Michael Sinclair: 126–27, 128–29 | Oberto Gili: 133 | Dominique Vorillon: 134 | Simon Upton/Interior Archive: 136 | Eric Piasecki/OTTO: 142–43, 166–67, 176 | Tim Beddow/The Interior Archive: 145 | Prue Roscoe: 158, 159 | Matthew Millman/Architectural Digest © Conde Nast: 177

Living Well by Design
First published in 2021 by The Vendome Press
Vendome is a registered trademark of The Vendome Press, LLC

NEW YORK
Suite 2043
244 Fifth Avenue
New York, NY 10001

LONDON
63 Edith Grove
London,
SW10 0LB, UK

www.vendomepress.com

Distributed in North America by Abrams Books
Distributed in the United Kingdom, and the rest of the world, by Thames & Hudson

ISBN 978-0-86565-395-5

Publishers: Beatrice Vincenzini, Mark Magowan, and Francesco Venturi
Editor: Jacqueline Decter
Production Director: Jim Spivey
Designer: Susi Oberhelman

Library of Congress Cataloging-in-Publication Data available upon request

Printed and bound in China by 1010 Printing International Ltd.
Second printing

PAGES 2-3: In a garden by landscape designer Paul Bangay, a pool house that looks as though it has always been there shares the same confident scale and design as a harbourside residence in Sydney designed by Thomas Hamel & Associates, Dylan Farrell Design, and Campbell Architecture.

PAGES 4-5: It's the details that make the difference between organized comfort and chaotic clutter. Whether the counters or the cookware, the flooring, or the furniture, you want things to last the distance, as in the classic marble kitchen at Wollumbi Estate in the Southern Highlands of New South Wales. Open racks are sometimes preferable to built-ins, as they don't shrink a room and can be used to fill an awkward niche and make stored items readily accessible.

PAGES 6-7: A beguiling alcove in the home of renowned travel writer Patrick Leigh Fermor and his wife, Joan, in Kardamyli, Greece. Built in the 1960s, it is now owned by the Benaki Museum and was recently renovated.

PAGES 8-9: In the courtyard of interior designer Michael Love's house in Sydney, beautifully trained vines clad the walls, bringing the outdoors in.

PAGES 10-11: In the tonally uniform entry hall at Wollumbi, an antique Italian statue mounted on a black plinth serves as a striking focal point.